KW-223-204

The Echoing Green

Also by Peter Levi

Peter Levi

The Echoing Green

THREE ELEGIES

Anvil Press Poetry

Published in 1983
by Anvil Press Poetry Ltd
69 King George Street London SE10 8PX

0 85646 111 3

Copyright © Peter Levi 1983

Printed in England by the
Arc & Throstle Press Todmorden Lancs

This book is published with
financial assistance from
The Arts Council of Great Britain

FOR DEIRDRE

CONTENTS

My title comes from two lines of Blake which I had misremembered as 'And shall no more be seen/Upon the echoing green.' The true version is 'And sport no more seen,/On the darkening Green.' But I find that 'The Ecchoing Green' was Blake's title for his poem. This series of three laments was written for three of my friends who died in 1981, all rather young for death. They were all scholars, and I had known them all in Oxford. Denis Bethell was a senior lecturer in medieval history at the National University of Ireland. He died of cancer. We were undergraduates at the same time in the nineteen fifties, and very close friends. I was already meditating his lament when Anne Pennington suddenly died, of a recurrence of the old cancer which had threatened her for many years. She was the newly elected Professor of Slavonic Philology at Oxford; she had been a fellow of Lady Margaret Hall. We had worked together at a series of translations, and she had become a close family friend, and a favourite visitor at Stonesfield, as Denis was. I had finished my lament for Denis and knew I would write one for Anne when at Christmas of 1981 Colin Macleod died by suicide. He was a classical scholar, my friend since he was a student, and in a sense my employer, since at that time I was working as his assistant and substitute at Christ Church where he was a tutor. Suicide is always private and often mysterious; that of Colin was utterly private. I have referred in the first part of his lament to Rugby and to Balliol, where he was educated, and in the second part to his own poems, which were published. In the lament for Denis Bethell, any allusions to our past will explain themselves. In the first part of the lament for Anne, I have referred to her rooms in her college, in the second part to her life in Yugoslavia and to her translations of Vasko Popa; the fifth part is an Easter sermon, because I had always promised to write her one. These three laments are a deliberate series of poems. Anne Pennington's is the Christian centre-piece, and Denis Bethell's is a pure elegy, a tribute of affection, but Colin Macleod's is the climax, it expresses unconsoled grief and unreconciled anger. They must be taken together.

For Denis Bethell

died 15 February 1981

I

Two swallows in the shed, the snow falling,
then the long days, the mysterious late year,
then low, low down over the withering hayfield
the young swallows swooping out of the air.

Memory is the ringing of the iron hooves of horses,
the turf thundering silent long ago,
the rampart of the downs stretching away in sunlight,
death was a distant willowshadow.

Angels with a few leaves hand in hand with the Muses
honour those long grasses and starlit bones
where an old saint's beard trails down out of heaven
and touches the black water into swans.

II

The shiver of the storm-light on the trees,
the coloured flowering of the dark trees,
and gleam of the cold grass under the trees,
speak of our greenish brown and swallow-skimmed
river of water in the sea of grass.
The dark wood-flowers ripened in the shade.
How cow-parsley smells heavy in the shade,

how light it is, grown up above the grass.
when three parts of the world are green and white.
In summer the dog panted in the shade.
Now the night-birds are quiet in the field
and the slow breath of the expiring fields
hangs on the night-air more roughly than mist.
The mountain drapes his ribs in dewy black
and stony smells like an unlevel field.
Dawn breaks as delicate as a dog-rose,
it drenches every field and mountainside.
All over. That is all over now.
The world was dying in his eyes dying,
summer and winter took ten years dying.
The yellow streaks were in the leaden sky,
he was not in the field, he was white bones
when three parts of this world were green and bright.

III

Walking at night retold the Odyssey
on gravel roads under the boughs of elms,
beyond the village houses chewed away
by water-streams and the rainfall of time.
The white deer in the forest of darkness,
and the white cattle on the lost island,
and the sad charcoal-coated deer pursued
through the dim wood between glimmering trees.
The yelling of a thousand birds at dawn.
The gentle treading of the feet of death.
A faint smell of an orange stuck with cloves.
We drank port and ate bacon sandwiches,
light found us washing in the empty Thames.

How long ago that is, how cold it is,
the air blowing today from that dark year.
Conversation I can no longer bear,
as innocent and formal as Shakespeare.
The Odyssey meandered on all night.

IV

The hill so clear and the field evergreen;
along the margins of the summer road
poppy here, crane's-bill there, that whistling like
the thistle-bearded fathers of our lives,
words nesting on roadsides like thistle-down.
There is a peace that sits on snowy hills,
a counterblast that cools the wit of man,
and something breathing on this summer road,
without a name, that had the tread of peace.
They, in their conversation mystical,
made time go backward, talking away time,
into a silver-fruited, bearded age,
while clear water ran onward in the brook
and the old fisherman bent to the brook:
and secret poachers in the darkest pools
fished scaly salmon by starlight alone.
These are the fathers of the British church,
black and grey are the colours of their words.
George Herbert's green breath was a dying breath,
green and white flowers sprout out of his death.
I praise my God, my God is all to me.
The never-ending non-sequiturs of the sea,
greener and whiter than George Herbert's grave,
salt-green, salt-white, console only the brave.

The seashore is where my life has ended.
The silver fruits have crumbled in my hand
Denis, and the white beards are blowing wild,
the Spirit has nested in the wild stones,
he sings terribly loudly in your bones.
When we were young we saw two lovers lie
embracing in a sunlit snowy field,
we thought them like two figures in John Donne.
We had not understood what human weight
John Donne dragged after him as poetry.
Whose heaven is the heaven of sermons,
sunday by sunday, snowfall by snowfall?
There are no lovers lying in that snow.
Our ghost of love has melted in that snow,
our ghost and our unstudied quietness.

V

Looms through the flashing mist the British isle.
The mist is sunstruck, the low cliff milkwhite,
and the green turning and returning sea
will loll and gasp away midsummer night.
May to December so easily runs,
and the machine of stars runs to ruin,
tugging the scholar from his bookish dark
and the cold mermaid under the salt sea.
The oracle silent a hundred years
in voices of the island watersprings,
our horse scars in the grass, two or three lines;
swallow and swift breed in the sunny sheds,
earth under beams is white with swallow-dung
and the deep walnut and the shooting plane

have their pleasure in sunlight and fine air.
Sun glitters on the plain glass of the church:
stone in flower by pure mathematics
which is the observation of nature.
Autumn in our lifetimes and the leaves fall,
the forest chapel is a pile of stones,
the leaves have dropped around your hermitage.
Neither the robin redbreast nor the wren
is busy now under the churchyard wall.
Who had the heart for building in our times?
Words for the true and good, words of the brave,
your building-stone paper under the lamp,
by the edge of the never silent sea.
The British islands swam like summer birds
in plumes of foam and slated plains of sea,
and they were generous in elements
and sang the music of their native stars
which they had learnt at their awakening.
Sleep Denis, the island is asleep
and in your heart the circle of our year
has ended in sleep and the fall of leaves.
The ocean rocks in its vast bed, the earth
is slowly heaving its green dragon scales
and it is time your world and mine should sleep.
And Izaak Walton's Lives sleep in their book,
a world that never lived until it died,
one that was pleasant on an old man's tongue
in holy conversations and good thoughts
and lingering irony like crab-apples.
I mean those scholars Walton thought should be
like Dukes in Shakespeare under the green bough.
Trees that were growing then are withered now.

15/

Only the sky at night is star-freckled
and the deep grass freckled with coloured weeds
draws the one sheet over all our white bones.

VI

Denis, I have been thinking of a world
that will go on for ever, never dies.
Grey and blue shadows and a waterfall,
between the thin trees in the winter sun;
treasures of autumn blacken underfoot,
winter will come then with amazing light.
It is the stream of water fresh on stone
and the thin forest in the early sun,
where the scholar of water and of stone
stood all night through in the devouring moon,
then like an owl mused as the world grew bright
pure yellow eyed in the blue winter light.
It is the spirit of our dying time
moving through shadows like an autumn stream.

16/

For Anne Pennington

died 27 May 1981

I

Early awake, a sunrise in treetops,
a million green feathers at tree height:
then on the garden floor the sun let fall
vast playing-cards of shadow and of light.

The shadows shifted, he played on and on;
his game of patience came out in the end,
and straggling shadows drowned in the deep dark,
the windows flamed and died for our one friend:

as if she walked outside under the trees
to hear a nightbird then lie down alone,
then talking to herself just one moment
she smiled as she was drowsing into stone.

II

All the blue distances have gone to sleep,
the quiet sun ripens above our heads
and still the sickle whispers in the wheat
and the scythe whistles in the grass on fire;
where are the white stones in the green meadow?
Ghost of a thunderbolt buzzing like bees
among the white ribs of our holy place,

17/

where the dew-sipping wolf will walk at dawn
and one bird shout in shadow at midday
whose whistle is rain-showers and earth-crumbs
and the slow swelling of fruit in the tree.
Where are you now in that big countryside?
who under the poor ruins of small domes
like shells that echoed in the ears of God
took honey from the dusty gold or dark,
a thousand and ten thousand days of stone.
So many blackbirds cry here at sunrise,
as if the sun had melted streaming down
to paint our frugal sky in tiny leaf:
the country of the senses, not the mind,
is food for the spirit, alive or dead.
Monasteries of towers in midair
crumble the sun to walls as white as snow,
brooding their passions among forest pines.

III

Roads of houses where the dead century
has been breathing quietly for so long
through blossoming branches and thin shadows,
there are so many patches of sunlight.
They fall on the pages of open books.
Architecture is the measure of man;
the tall white colleges disrobe themselves
to see their own beauties in floodwater;
they were the decoration of your soul
Anne, when they clapped their white wings in your mind;
and their nature was living in your mind,
the momentum of so much quietness.

Then the long snowy discipline of books,
austerities of maplewood music,
the one string of the Serbian Iliad:
winter marsh-birds inviting to darkness
and the self-conversation of spirit:
a groan of breath like a chant in heaven.

IV

I will go to the temple of my god,
arbour of darkness, leaf-house at midnight,
the leaden goddess of a sea of grass,
Britannia in shadow of the moon,
or in the sheds when swallows house or when
the silver sun in blue liquidity
kindles the heavy-smelling forest light
and the wild sow moves in the darker trees;
darkness is the refreshment of my soul,
it is in rivers running below trees.
How fast they ran, how obscure in our time
all day and night through solitudes of grass
and meadow flowers that revived in rain.
Anne, when you swam there sleeker than a bird,
salmon glided all day under those streams,
and ghostly water-creatures, green sea-crabs
that flock to feed or bask on Danube sand
praised heaven with the goddess of waters.
Now your white ash is resting among trees,
and the long lake lapping at mist and rock
sighs to the mountain and the mountain sighs.
June has melted with his dissolving swans
where ragged willows mark the edge of Thames,

the rank haymeadows have withered away
and the sunset is yellow in the sky.

V

Deuteronomy 4, 11

The mountain burns with fire in midheaven
with darkness and with cloud and thick darkness:
the voice of God, ash on the burnt mountain,
as light as the white spray on the green sea.
Our God, but we have known him otherwise,
spirit in conversation with spirit
in fainting light and in blue morning light
when crimson and white blossom stood in trees,
speaking in Galilee beside the lake:
the voice of ash in the breaking of bread.
The mountain burns with fire in midheaven,
the earth is fresh now and the spirit speaks,
the sea is silver-scaled and thistle-green,
the mountain drowzes among apricots.
Our sun rises as clear as crystal stone,
the voice in the white spray on the green thorn
is bird music and the voice of spirit
is loud, it will never be lost or die:
because immortal Easter fills our soul,
as you knew your own soul and were silent.
Death gave gravity to Jesus Christ,
and all our souls drown in his death and blood,
because he drooped his holy head to sleep
and suffered and in shadows was refreshed,
as the ascending lark from his rough bed

climbs in the sight of heaven's sparkling sun.
When he let fall the cold dew of his death
having become what we were in his life
and spoke with the last gravity of love,
his dying spirit entered your soul then,
and when his sunrise step out of his sleep
trod down the tatters of our soul's darkness,
the green side of the sleeping mountain broke,
fresh water ran, the mountain of God woke,
and your soul whispered and the spirit spoke.
Angels in heaven that will never die
sprinkle larksong in the pale early sky
over the shepherd of eternity.
The lark ascending when Christ has risen
is your mind on any simple morning,
and the chorus at dawn in blushing light
and the last bird calling through evening light
repeat the happy wishes of childhood;
mysterious trees flower deep in the wood.
Because Christ is risen and his mountain
is streaming water and will never die,
and we are overshadowed by his tree.
Spirit or star chiming one silver note
Anne you are singing of the son of God
meditated in the breaking of bread.

VI

How slow the wind is in river meadows,
the book of suns is too lazy to close:
flowers ripen without any movement,
the shadow of the oak tree is silent,

there is something Chinese in this long light,
the deep grass at midday as fresh as night,
and the cold water's light changeable note
quietly lapping while the heavy boat
sways among dragonflies as blue as air.
The river-weeds have let loose their green hair,
and all of this, windshadow and birdbreath
are somehow full of peacefulness and death.
It is the image of your quietness;
no one has ever troubled the light less,
being so deep and so silent, as though
a life lived is an hour in a meadow.

For Colin Macleod

died 18 December 1981

I

Chapels in colleges and shabby squares
generate no spirit but a faint breeze,
darkness squeezes the lemon juice of light,
night disquiets dead leaves under our trees.

It has all gone to seed now, it has run down,
just city delicate as a hare-bone,
cloister or temple in the mind of man;
water is harder in the end than stone.

The gods of the body do not exist,
beyond this time there lies another one:
monastic chapel, or old Roman square
with colours that have drained out of the sun.

II

What else is God or the bright eye of God
but fire that flickers if it is alight?
If heaven is tawny like a desert:
a waste of sand-hill where no weed will shoot,
combed over by sun-shadows or the wind.
And this is the pure garden of the soul.
What other pride is proper in God's eye

than the refusal to be comforted?
Something shattered in the heart of the sun
has mingled into green rivers of light,
our cool planet will never be silent,
birdmusic is loud and intractable,
and when the sun rises into wet air
and when the sun sinks out of dry air
the sea's surface is noisy by nature:
but the communication of spirit
walks in the desert haunted by one word
springing to die on the lips of silence.

III

Scholars of art, teachers by trade, dare not
pray for a field of grass: Muses go by,
the humorous classics will not permit.
A life that filters poetry through sleep
returns it through dream to a dream-like life:
in our life one page was alive again
Colin, the Roman garden, the hill farm,
rough grazing and the air-shadowing trees,
wild creeping herbs, nanny-goat smells, pine fires,
mountain water and a shell of clean salt.
You felt the loss before the thing, the sun
fell hissing and the world sank like a kite:
we will stray after it over the edge
beyond moist earth and our own earth's goddess,
das Ewig-weibliche, our brief pleasure;
nothing natural knows any owner.
Then came days when the sun bloomed softly
on the misty skin of the dark grape

and the glittering skin of the dark sea,
but your eyes burned like a star that will die
and your brain smouldered like a garden fire
breathing death twenty years before it died.
Courage to live at all is our one pride.

IV

Rainbow-streak, the wind-footed messenger,
leaping down from a storm to the dark sea
landed between a few rocky islands:
the deep water groaned under the weight.
Dawn blushes with Homeric irony.
Tired gods are crunching old human head-bones,
they will not give up earthly poetry.
They will take away the shadow of the trees,
they will take it
they will take from you the shadow of the sea
they will take it
they will take the shadow of the heart they will take it
they will take away your shadow.
Seferis and Homer, both terrible:
the sea was their father
green and unripe and heaving between rocks
and groaning like a bed with broken springs
fretting to foam around each island,
cold as a fresh leaf shooting on the vine.
Seal and seawoman mated in the sea
round the moist marge of your cold Hebrid isle.
Fresh voices chanted in the crumbling sea,
green frozen fire dripping into white ash
and piping birds beside the sea's margin:

the infinite lake sighing and splashing:
voices without sunlight, moonlight, starlight
in the cold cave of your nativity.
Therefore nature's great minister the sun
imprinting heaven in receiving earth
crops what it rears, and the moisture of earth
in the moon's circle cries and cannot rise;
a poet lives and dies where heaven's eye dies.
His blood whispers as coldly as starlight
and the cold whisper of the stone seacave.
Now is time Colin for the ocean's edge
and lamentation of the island sea
Atlantic wind, ironic wild sea-birds,
the sea's dewfall that freezes away time,
the moon's dewfall that freezes away time.

V

Spring was monotonously brilliant:
summers of failure, brilliant and dumb,
hope like autumnal sunlight between trees,
winter will come.
One uncontainable deep grieving rage
sweeps through the wood and the last leaves let go:
sky full of death, wind blast, one iron taste,
one fall of snow.
Twenty five years before your time my dear
I have laid my head down on railway lines
but it was in a dream of future time,
it withered and the sun wears away thoughts.
The last time I saw you the snowy wind
was already beginning to blow,

and I can feel your rage in the snow wind,
insulted courage, insulted spirit:
the god himself will free me when I will,
meaning death, death is the last line.
Then when you died the fellows in their gowns
ran cawing like a colony of rooks
disturbed in airy quadrangles of stone,
and like those crows that roared in the rigging
and roosted on Apollo's temple roof
when the bell tolled for Cicero to die;
they flapped wings, tugged his bedding with their beaks:
then slaves carried him fast to the seashore:
noise of men running: sea roared, crows roared:
they caught him in his narrow garden walks.
He was betrayed of course. And deserted
because the black crows are Apollo's birds.
He stuck his head unshaven and his long
scrawny old neck well out from his litter.
They killed him, then cut off his hand and tongue.
And now the crows are cawing in Plutarch,
dark writing in the edges of your life,
ominous as Apollo in our times:
I will build up Apollo's garden shrine
rethinking and rethinking of your death.
How clear the sky is in your poetry:
suffering of spirit that refuses
all consolation delusion or drug
and will ride through clear blue as the sun does;
the crows have made their colony in me,
they confuse my hearing, I cannot see
from end to end of my philosophy.
I can hear your titanic lonely cry,

fortitude, the last gate of privacy.
Happy the man who lives among heroes,
for their cry of defiance will live on
wherever men have ears to hear that cry.

VI

The full season comes to rest at high tide
when the wild sorrel rusts on the roadside,
it is a road you have often taken
or like a place long known, long forgotten:
under the rough fingers of chestnut trees
or where the wood squanders its mysteries.
Words finish, though the closing notes drag on,
I live among things past their true season:
God has crumbled the stars in his own sky,
nothing is breathing but antiquity,
our world is broken, it lies where it fell,
under the crust earth is an iron bell
heaving its awful weight around the sky:
it is swinging and clanging silently.
I say your likeness is to an old stone:
upright, raineaten, mooneaten, alone.